HouseBeautiful

TABLESCAPES

HouseBeautiful

TABLESCAPES

SETTING A STYLISH TABLE

LISA CREGAN

HEARST
books

CONTENTS

FOREWORD

What could be lovelier than the act of setting a table? China plain or patterned, fine metals glinting, cloth to hold, crystal or cut-glass to clink, and the doodads, oh the doodads!—from napkin rings to salt cellars. To say nothing of flowers! The idea of arranging a medley of beautiful objects into a memorable experience merits a moniker: *tablescape*. Anyone can place a fork to the left and the drinking glass to the right, but it takes a passionate host to add a charger or a brass pheasant or a hand-written place card that one guest might tuck away and save for a lifetime.

Tablescapes embody all the elements I love about home design. They're a microcosm of style at our fingertips and there's the chance to create one three times a day—four if you take teatime! Unlike redecorating a room, the task isn't too daunting, yet it's infinitely variable, and always presents a reward: to enhance a shared moment between you and guests, to honor your partner or your family with a small gesture, or to simply remind yourself to *slow down* and be. I for one light candles when I dine solo! Don't wait for a holiday or even dinnertime. Open a page, seize on an idea, and ready, SET, go . . . you're on your way to a more beautiful life.

Sophie Donelson

Editor in Chief, *House Beautiful*

CHAPTER ONE

A VERY CIVILIZED AFFAIR

THERE'S NOTHING WRONG WITH A LITTLE FORMALITY NOW AND THEN.

IT GIVES YOU LICENSE TO PULL OUT ALL THE STOPS AND

PUT YOUR PERSONAL STAMP ON A VERY SPECIAL NIGHT.

PLUS, YOU GET TO USE ALL YOUR FANCIEST FINERY!

≪ Don't let a little thing like home renovation cramp your style. Why not give an eccentric spin to your down-to-the-studs construction site? How about taper candles in plastic shower knobs and a heavily bleached painter's drop cloth for a tablecloth? Renovation is hard; dinner parties are fun.

⌃ Pattern overload is kept in check by strict adherence to the dining chairs' color palette. Old and new are interwoven, with heirloom sterling getting a refreshing jolt from a mix of gold flatware. To top it off, a calligrapher created the menus on work-order forms!

(Previous Spread) Fearless femininity is channeled by a soft turquoise, pink, and brown palette. Tucking a single flower bud into each napkin adds yet another chic couture moment.

« Formal but also playful? It can be done. Taking cues from the flame-pattern dining chairs, these robin's-egg-blue glass goblets and turquoise placemats are happy foils for a riotous centerpiece.

˅ A bit of tropical punch—paradise gone luxe—can lift the spirit even in the dead of winter. Set a table with gilded pineapples and palm baubles to evoke balmy breezes. It's like a one-way ticket to Mustique.

"BE PRETTY IF YOU CAN. BE WITTY IF YOU MUST. BUT BE GRACIOUS IF IT KILLS YOU."

ELSIE DE WOLFE

A profusion of pink flowers and green glass goblets (a winning color combination) play off the blues in the dining room's shimmering chinoiserie-papered walls. The setting avoids a too-formal edge with playful ceramic foo dogs. ≫

THE ULTIMATE DRESSY DINNER

⌄   Somehow, blue-and-white stripes make everything seem more lighthearted. So even though the table is laid with sterling silver flatware (the spoon above the plate is for dessert) and the linen napkins are starched and monogrammed, no one's going to fret over picking up the wrong fork.

»   Contemporary Venetian glasses mix beautifully with classically patterned dishes and silverware. Instead of a single large flower arrangement, bouquets are grouped in containers in the center of the table, with the whole elegant array set before playful nineteenth-century scenic wallpaper.

>> Lavender bouquets—
and goblets to match—
emphasize a feeling of
perpetual spring in this
country dining room.
Nailhead-studded chair
backs, embroidered
curtains, and a natural
fiber rug add a note of
texture to the room's
visual symphony.

THE ULTIMATE DRESSY DINNER

⌄ A collection of Irish decanters filled with aged bourbon moves easily from sideboard to table for an after-dinner tipple.

» Antique china along with chinoiserie candlesticks make this table a glorious throwback to a more formal era. Knives are propped on ornate knife rests, a grace note that's overdue for a revival.

« A blazing red library featuring a pillow-bedecked Chinese daybed is transformed into an exotic dinner spot by the addition of a few colorful dining chairs. Gathering up the side of the red damask tablecloth gives the table the flamboyance of a bustle-skirted ball gown.

⩟ Pairing a rustic rattan charger with an antique ceramic bowl creates a playful contrast, and the inexpensive linen dish towel embellished with an elaborate monogram adds another unexpected twist to the tabletop. A variety of delightful objets, like an elephant vase set amid a forest of bright blue glassware, provide one cheery burst of life after another.

"AFTER A GOOD DINNER ONE CAN FORGIVE ANYBODY, EVEN ONE'S OWN RELATIVES."

OSCAR WILDE

Tidying up after dinner is a very pretty job when the dessert service features a collection of colorful vintage china. But don't be in a hurry. Too often, the fun gets cleared away with the plates. Linger! »

THE ULTIMATE DRESSY DINNER

⌄ To deliver a wow factor, embroidered placemats (for texture) are layered over a lustrous fuchsia mat (for a bright pop of color), and the whole affair is set off by a white burlap tablecloth. An ombré napkin picks up all the colors in the setting to knit the palette together.

≫ The hosts of a large dinner party create intimacy via a tabletop teeming with bibelots, candles, and flowers. Jaw-snapping alligator napkin rings lurk amid the abundance of brio—including birds' nests filled with pansies and a troop of white porcelain monkeys.

« A dinner party becomes a floribunda fantasy when the table is set up in a greenhouse and features a centerpiece composed entirely of porcelain flowers.

⩔ The marine-blue tablecloth provides dramatic contrast to the gilt interior of the Jefferson cups—silver tumblers with gold interiors originally designed in 1787 by Thomas Jefferson himself. Pewter chargers add to the setting's presidential appeal.

« The taxidermy peacock on the sideboard casts a romantic spell over this dining room, where menu cards and place cards signal to guests that they're in for a very special evening.

⌄ A polished place setting worthy of a big anniversary hews strictly to its palette of glittering silvers, grays, and whites. The most jaw-dropping touch, though, is the waterfall of creamy roses and hydrangeas spilling from a hollowed-out birch log.

"STYLE—
ALL WHO HAVE IT
SHARE ONE THING:
ORIGINALITY."

DIANA VREELAND

« Want to talk audacity? How about simply taking whatever's in season at the local farmers' market and making it the centerpiece of your lavish dinner party? In this case, sturdy red-veined rhubarb stalks fill a vase, and an armload of pomegranates are strewn across the table. To top it off, hammered silver flatware flagrantly breaks the "don't mix your metals" rule by congenially rubbing elbows with brass candleholders and gold-lettered place cards.

A stimulating table with lots of eye-catching detail is always appetizing. Here, mixed and matched candlesticks steal the show. Graphic patterned plates and the punctuation of small bouquets complete this very personal table. Note the watercolor place cards popped into each bowl.

Pink and green has never looked less preppy than it does here. Venetian glass goblets pair grandly with antique seafoam-green rimmed plates, all surrounding an aging antique *tulipiere* studded with purple roses.

"I DIM THE LAMPS AND USE SO MANY CANDLES YOU FEEL LIKE YOU'RE INSIDE A SNIFTER OF BRANDY HELD UP TO THE FIRE."

MILES REDD

Break the ice with a uniquely personal table. Geometric-shaped plates rest on a tablecloth that resembles rolled molten gold. White flowers keep the brighter hues in check, while the black table runner and placemats add a hit of gravitas. »

THE ULTIMATE DRESSY DINNER

» There's no dining room more glamorous than one glittering and aglow. Supersized gold mint julep cups, filled with purple clematis, reference burnished brass chairs. And plates placed directly atop the table ensure the sparkly reflection of the highly polished wood isn't buried beneath a tablecloth.

» When you want to go all-out romantic, set your table on a field of lavender. Purple sweet peas mix with bouquets of wide-eyed white anemones and mirrored hurricane lamps. White plates topped with blue linen napkins throw sparks of light that pop happily off the table.

« Delicately tinted crystal is the perfect way to add fantasy without overpowering the table. This setting is a curvaceous, opalescent, pastel delight. Luxurious Venetian glass is lightheartedly offset by the occasional ceramic insect skittering its way across the tablecloth, which is itself embroidered with the silhouettes of place settings.

⌄ A glass collection glows on a windowsill, awaiting its next employment in some magical dinner table vignette.

≪ Classic cut-glass crystal goblets and good china look smart on crisp navy placemats. And just a few simple hydrangeas (even the local grocery-store variety) in classic Chinese ginger jars can elevate a place setting to sophisticated perfection.

⩓ Light dances around this city terrace table with its iridescent taffeta tablecloth and shimmering cut-glass lantern centerpiece. Set against a mirrored lattice backdrop, dinner becomes a sparkling treat.

43

A SIMPLY ELEGANT EVENING

The humble cabbage has been a favored porcelain motif for centuries. Here, it's elegantly employed to create a "winter white" garden table. Creamy leaf plates and an ivory compote on white linens offer neutral touches amid the embellishment of fresh produce and green roses.

Centerpieces are low-slung so diners can easily talk across them, and chairs are purposely grouped close together so every guest feels a part of the conversation.

"I SAY, BUY BEAUTIFUL PLATES AND PUT THEM IN THE DISHWASHER. I USE MY SILVER EVERY DAY, SO IT DOESN'T EVEN NEED TO BE POLISHED."

BUNNY WILLIAMS

« A collection of old silver and antiqued mercury glass readily at hand means you can arrange a glittering dinner party as quickly as you can order your favorite takeout.

⌃ A crisp monochromatic setting is devoid of fussiness but loaded with style. Here the china's border—classic platinum edging—is emphasized by a silver ice bucket and sterling flatware. Napkins placed on a bare tabletop were given just a very light press to ensure they stay in a natural state, and wine goblets are sturdy, not fragile.

⏩ Silver and glass are always a glamorous pair. Here, sensuous glass shapes—from candlesticks to a fishbowl filled with floating magnolias—play off silver goblets and mirrors to create the most flattering reflective light. Every diner's face is illuminated by candlelight glinting from the collection of sparkling surfaces.

>> A vivacious wallpaper is all that's needed to get the party started in this dining room. Visual power comes from both coral-colored napkins and tiny vases filled with ranunculus that play up the lotus and carp motif sheathing the room. Gold goblets echo the brass chandelier, and dark plates harmonize with the steel sideboard.

"PART OF THE PLEASURE OF ENTERTAINING IS DREAMING UP ALL THE LITTLE THINGS THAT MAKE THE NIGHT FEEL SPECIAL."

JANE SCOTT HODGES

A table set for a big dinner transforms a raw industrial space into an utterly charming spot for celebration. Pastel colors, as seen in the pale yellow roses and pink bowls, soften the feel of white steel chairs, while mercury-glass candlesticks reflect the romantic glow from the ornate crystal chandelier. »

« Anyone can seem a flower-arranging genius simply by using a single variety of flower per vase. Utilizing multiple containers of varying heights creates every bit as much drama as a large (and expensive) multibloom centerpiece from the florist.

⌄ A flowered bowl looks great on this geometric plate, thanks to the strict blue-and-white palette that governs the entire setting. Placing votives on a silver tray doubles the effect of the candlelight, and matching glasses and tumblers enhance the visual rhythm of the table.

A SIMPLY ELEGANT EVENING

⩔ Wild blooms set on a neutral milk-and-honey palette make flowers the guests of honor. Raspberry cuttings and dill weed add a hint of the wild to the dahlia arrangements.

» Stacked creamware plates showcase only the food and its bounty of color, yet the china's beaded edging adds a touch of textural interest. The tablecloth has a very subtle pattern to create warmth and depth beneath plain linen napkins.

« Wood + Stone + Flowers = Perfection. Being surrounded by nature is grounding, and you can never go wrong with a neutral setting and all-white flowers. The tree looks like it's grown right out of the table, creating a canopy, while the moss runner softens the vast expanse of wood.

⌃ Handcrafted pasta bowls are mellow enough for every day but pretty enough for guests. The matte white china mixes beautifully with these glossy gray pieces. Soft earth colors, stubbly textured napkins, and clear glass vases filled with daisies are the embodiment of organic elegance.

THE EXTRAVAGANT HOLIDAY SOIREE

>> The icy colors of this open-plan apartment are made party-ready by inviting in the warm notes of the centerpiece's red blooms.

⋎ A round placemat adds a contrasting layer atop the mahogany table, and a linen napkin will always feel special when lightly starched, pressed, and folded. Sets of salt and pepper cellars scattered around the table are easy for guests to reach. Place cards attached to a small gift add the spirit of generosity to a holiday table.

"THERE IS NOTHING IN THE WORLD SO IRRESISTIBLY CONTAGIOUS AS LAUGHTER AND GOOD HUMOR."

CHARLES DICKENS

Let it snow, let it snow, let it snow. Especially when you're wrapped in the warmth of your nearest and dearest beside a roaring fire. Isn't that what the holidays are all about? Gathering family and friends in a congenial environ where everyone can shine. A soft-spoken silver-and-white table and loose floral arrangements (and a carafe of good red wine) ensure your guests' stories will be heard above the decor—but do note the subtle flourish of the twig flatware and botanical leaf napkin rings. »

THE EXTRAVAGANT HOLIDAY SOIREE

⌄ A blizzard of humongous paper snowflakes makes for a maximalist's notion of wintry fun. Objects of different heights add a sense of intimacy—the snowflakes bring the high ceiling down, while the towering candlesticks lift the table skyward.

» Vases twinkle while wood candlesticks pull warmth from the brick mantelpiece. At the holidays, the olive branch, an emblem of peace, takes on special meaning when used as a fireplace garland. It also has a subtle fragrance that adds another layer of interest to the room.

"THAT'S WHAT LIFE IS ALL ABOUT: LET'S HAVE A PARTY. LET'S HAVE IT TONIGHT."

LILLY PULITZER

« This party started with the menu—squash soup—and a yellowy orange color palette followed. The bright color of the linen placemats harmonizes with the explosion of orchids and sets a fiery tone for the table. Amber tumblers add warmth to cool drinks on a cold winter night, and when the guests lift the lids of their individual tureens, a delicious aroma fills the room.

THE EXTRAVAGANT HOLIDAY SOIREE

⋎   A jubilant table set for a big holiday dinner party glistens with quirky objects like a meandering pair of antique silver pheasants. The tablecloth's subtle pattern lends a wonderful texture to the setting, and a vintage silver punchbowl centerpiece strains to corral ranunculus, hellebores, bittersweet, and amaryllis. The pashminas elegantly tied around each chair back are gifts to the guests.

»   Instead of the traditional red-and-green palette, metals are mixed for glittery appeal. Layered plates of various shapes add up to a rich and eclectic setting, and the immaculate pale seafoam-green napkins are an unexpected update on standard white.

⌃ Yes, a custom-made tablecloth that echoes the wallpaper is an extravagance, but one totally worthy of a big holiday celebration. Decanters of red wine match the opulent shade of crimson in the abundant bouquets of red roses.

≫ Traditional plates and classic silver marry with the timeless formality of the setting. A napkin tucked beneath the plate lets guests enjoy an unobstructed view of the intricate china pattern.

"DON'T TAKE
YOURSELF
TOO SERIOUSLY.
ANYTHING GOES
THESE DAYS
WITH YOUR TABLE
DECOR AND MENU,
SO HAVE FUN."

TOBI FAIRLEY

What a delight to sit down to dinner with this gaggle of birch-bark wild animals. Pinecones and cut boughs complete the woodland effect. With heirloom china, colored glass goblets, and horn-handled utensils, it's nothing short of wintertime magic. »

CHAPTER TWO

KEEPING IT CASUAL

KICKING BACK WITH YOUR CLOSEST PALS IS WHAT THE GOOD LIFE IS ALL ABOUT, RIGHT? BUT A LOW-KEY DRESS CODE DOESN'T MEAN YOUR GATHERING CAN'T BE OVER-THE-TOP PRETTY. GO FOR IT!

《 A mix of rustic and refined elements pleases the eye. Glazed terra-cotta plates mingle with artisanal glassware. Mismatched plates personalize the setting for each guest, while purple placemats and bold orange napkins create a spicy palette that hints at a flavorful dinner to come.

(Previous Spread) Stoneware plates and handblown goblets add a simple elegance to the rustic ten-foot-long table that welcomes guests to this vegetable and cutting garden. The scale of the enormous vase filled with Queen Anne's lace—which too many consider a weed!—gives it the refined presence of sculpture.

∧ Fearlessly rich color, like magenta dahlias in glossy black vases, mixes with the burly texture of chunky placemats on a muscular table and the bright flash of turquoise plates. It makes a snug spot for a happy home-style meal.

SUNDAY SUPPER

⩔ In a dining room with only picture lights, it falls to candles to play up the colorful soup tureen and the room's quirky poultry theme. Antique black Hitchcock chairs offset the snappy yellow-and-white tablecloth.

≫ On a cool summer evening, a romantically ramshackle old pub table is set on a screened porch. Glossy red-and-white plates with gray chargers contrast with the texture of the table's hard-won patina. Finishing off the sensuous scene took nothing more than some simple succulents.

"FOOD IS SYMBOLIC OF LOVE WHEN WORDS ARE INADEQUATE."

ALAN D. WOLFELT

Is there anything more sublime than Sunday night by the fire? And what could be more "stopping by woods" cozy than a buffalo-check napkin paired with floral plates? A hurricane lamp on an antiqued table between two wing chairs creates an intimate scene for a pair of country lovers. »

≪ Since there's nothing more fitting in the evening than candlelight, why not group candlesticks together and watch your party catch fire? Smoky gray glassware blends into the background, while an ornate lantern and arrangements on pedestals draw the eye.

⌄ Dinner for two—by lamplight. A lamp is an elegant yet homey alternative to candles (as long as it's on a dimmer!). A simple arrangement keeps this intimate dinner free from fussiness. Chic and simple proves flair isn't about the grand flourish.

‹‹ Two exotic tropical flowers in a plain glass vase lift a simple Sunday meal to the level of a feast. Blue rims take everyday dinner plates up a notch, and a bowl of pears finishes off the luscious look.

SUNDAY SUPPER

⌄ Apartment living often means no dining-room table, or at least not one big enough for entertaining. How about installing an enormous coffee table instead? A cherry blossom centerpiece gives height to the low-slung setting, while kumquats and artichokes add bursts of color. For a repast featuring that city dwellers' staple of takeout Chinese, guests perch on folding stools with chopsticks at the ready on glass butterfly stands.

» Plates with a "cupped hands" motif look as if they're personally presenting each guest a precious bowl. A soup spoon with a classic Chinese motif peeks out of a linen napkin tied with a red tassel.

"CROWD THE TABLE A LITTLE: WITH MORE PEOPLE AT THE TABLE NO ONE CAN IGNORE THEIR NEIGHBOR."

ANDREW FISHER

Silver candelabra for dining en famille? Why not? Creating the right mood puts everyone in a good one. A breeze blows in through French doors, and the flicker of candles illuminates fresh picked flowers. Bear-shaped salt and pepper shakers reference this home's mountainside location. ❯❯

« Pink cosmos from the farmers' market and iron lanterns bring a rustic spirit to a kitchen table casually set with bowls for Sunday-night stew.

⌃ In a house where the kitchen doubles as dining room, crimson peonies along with pomegranates and apples match the blood-red painting that dominates the space—guests forget they're dining in the kitchen because the focus is on the art.

⌄ Game night is sexy and chic when the table is set with metallic pops to add a bit of glamour. Shimmering accents like stemware with wide gold rims, contemporary gold flatware, and chunky gilded napkin rings are balanced by matte black-and-white plates. Simple magnolia leaves in a tall vase are all that's needed to complete a winning setting.

» Chicken potpies on a carved flip-top game table, simple tea towels for napkins, a single red peony, and a bottle of burgundy (don't forget the wine coaster!) are an oh-so-civilized way to wind down the weekend.

≪ A spirited blue, white, and yellow color combination is perfect for a convivial afternoon lunch. Mixing clear with colored glass creates visual depth, and ordinary grocery-store flowers make impossibly chic centerpieces with the blooms all cut to the same height and packed tightly into plain white bowls.

⟫ Antique china is used in a very contemporary way. The clean lines of modern wood-handled utensils offset ornate porcelain, and tumblers with rattan holders are another casual note. Vintage linens were hand-dyed to give them a fresh feel.

«« The dining room's high-spirited colors—light pink, chartreuse, and magenta—are echoed by a fantastical hydrangea centerpiece and richly hued glass hurricane lamps. Simple black-and-white place settings introduce contrast and make the palette read even more bold and exuberant.

97

˅ When your curtains are this cheerful and bright, why not match the mood with a big statement—like an enormous turquoise vase at the center of your table? Lush red-and-white dahlias are a foil for pristine midcentury-modern decor.

≫ Pull up a tray! Design your place settings in the kitchen, and enlist your guests to tote them to the table. Cleanup is simply the reverse! Tall topiaries emphasize the high ceiling, and a red Indian-print tablecloth harmonizes with red striped plates.

WEEKEND LUNCH WITH FRIENDS

⌄ An exotic Moroccan luncheon is delicious to look at, too. A mix of blue-and-white patterns in plates, napkins, and tablecloth makes for a lovely laid-back vibe. Natural rattan lanterns and chargers lend touchable warmth.

» Red is the natural opposite of blue, so the flowers literally pop off the tablecloth, and the centerpiece lends drama to the deep blue-colored glass. The orderly geometry of the napkin design ties all the assorted blue-and-white patterns together.

"THIS IS THE POWER OF GATHERING; IT INSPIRES US, DELIGHTFULLY, TO BE MORE HOPEFUL, MORE JOYFUL, MORE THOUGHTFUL: IN A WORD, MORE ALIVE."

ALICE WATERS

Even a party of four for lunch feels special when a profusion of parrot tulips spills from the heart of the table. Green tumblers and green glass plates call out the colors of the little wrapped gifts that provide a surprise for guests when they take their seats. »

WEEKEND LUNCH WITH FRIENDS

⌄ Fall colors add colorful snap to a blue-and-white tablecloth, and green dishes make everything and anything served on them look appetizing. A pair of antler candlesticks catches the eye and makes the table feel seasonally special.

» A pink theme and iridescent chargers bring a rosy glow to a daytime table. Ranunculus and roses placed loosely in a modern champagne flute have a friendly attitude, and utensils rest haphazardly on linen napkins, giving the whole setting a sit-back-and-relax vibe.

WEEKEND LUNCH WITH FRIENDS

⌄ This unruly collage of colors and patterns somehow meshes beautifully because, even though the plates vary from seat to seat, the napkins, chargers, and placemats are uniform, holding chaos at bay.

» Improvise! A little cactus or succulent in a brass tube cap from the hardware store makes a cute bit of swag to send home with your guests. A wide blue velvet ribbon makes a great stand-in for a table runner, and a drinking glass with gold details doubles as a vase.

≪ A turquoise hue is boldly pulled from a favorite painting for both glassware and vase simultaneously, adding interest to the artwork and the setting. The tablecloth feels like cascading leaves and creates a lush landscape in the dining room.

≫ High-energy colors make everyone feel good. Electric blue, neon orange, *and* hot pink? Follow the bliss with bright vivid goblets, lime-green napkins, and orange resin flatware on a lively patterned tablecloth. An African-mask napkin ring completes the wild affair.

« A breeze off the water blows life into this luncheon table. Blue pairs beautifully with the color of the sea, and shells and coral are simply a must-do this close to the ocean. But this setting actually started with the cabbage plates, which inspired the mounded vegetable centerpiece.

^ Mini champagne bottles with colorful drinking straws put an adult spin on a childlike pleasure. Summer zephyrs conjure thoughts of spreading towels on the sand for impromptu picnics, so why not use a beach towel like this one for a tablecloth? Wood-handled flatware adds another touch of natural warmth, and a bandanna is a fun stand-in for a linen napkin.

« Quiet beauty reigns when a willowy antique French campaign table is set with coral and an explosion of friendly daisies. Soft-blue glass plates match the color of the napkins to complete the feeling of easy serenity.

⋎ Relax, it's only lunch! And if you (and your table) look calm, guests will enjoy themselves that much more. Linens are left unstarched to look natural, and simple agapanthus blooms arranged in drinking glasses feel very off-the-cuff. A sideboard keeps extra dishes and napkins within easy arm's reach.

≪ Giant seashell soup bowls dish up the drama, while amber hurricanes soften the scene with a gentle glow.

⌄ Under this sumptuous wisteria-laden arbor, all the table needs is compotes cascading with luscious grapes to complete the lavish setting. The chandelier was custom-made to hold candles, which add a fairy-tale flicker to the scene.

TWILIGHT ON THE TERRACE

˅ A parade of potted herbs marches down the center of a table set for an alfresco summer dinner. The hand-blocked botanical-print tablecloth provides a joyful bridge between the convivial tabletop and the surrounding garden.

›› Subtly gold-rimmed chargers let green glass plates become dramatic standouts. A terra-cotta French faience pot is repurposed as an ice bucket for wine because, unlike glass or silver, it won't leave beads of water on the tablecloth.

"GLAMOROUS INFORMALITY IS THE NAME OF THE GAME. DRESS UP, EVEN IF YOU ARE SERVING HOT DOGS!"

SIMON DOONAN

Top a cocktail table with Moroccan tile and you've instantaneously gained a romantic spot for an outdoor meal. A black-and-white palette adds a touch of the urbane and plays up the many shades of green spilling over the garden wall. »

≪ Palm leaves part like lily pads for a curious green ceramic carp, creating a scene that harmonizes perfectly with its watery tropical-island setting. A coral tablecloth and purple tumblers keep the mood vibrant and lively even after the sun goes down.

⌄ Layer upon layer of interest creates an outdoor table worthy of its lush landscape. A napkin folded into an interesting shape (search online for ideas and how-tos) adds a small extravagance without going over the top.

TWILIGHT ON THE TERRACE

It's hard to compete with the golf-course views framed by this octagonal dining porch, but pink placemats the color of the sky at sunset are able to pull it off.

High and low have a dinner date: fancy china, heirloom silver . . . and plastic glasses.

MORNING GLORY BRUNCH

◀◀ A milk-glass vase filled with an explosion of poppies calls out the red flowers in the wallpaper and serves as a much healthier wake-up than a double shot of espresso. This is a table that will really get the adrenaline flowing for the day ahead.

⌄ Starting the morning with eye candy like a *faux bois* plate on an orange-striped runner, special spoons to crack your soft-boiled eggs, and ivory-enameled knives for the jam and strawberries? That's going to make the whole day go well.

MORNING GLORY BRUNCH

This breezy blue-and-white themed brunch springs from its surprising plaid tablecloth. Mixing in floral-patterned napkins and some splashy amethyst candlesticks creates a treat even for tired eyes.

The high-gloss gleam of lacquered kitchen cabinets reflects on an array of breakfast delicacies (egg cups are such an old-fashioned delight). And who wouldn't want to come down to breakfast greeted by a profusion of pink flowers in a footed mercury-glass vase?

"ALL HAPPINESS DEPENDS ON A LEISURELY BREAKFAST."

JOHN GUNTHER

≪ When in New Orleans, do as the natives do—give a Mardi Gras breakfast featuring a yellow can of pure cane syrup (served without ceremony on a tray amid the roses). Locals pour it indiscriminately over their biscuits and pancakes. The hand-strung beads have name tags attached, and woven rush-grass mats take the place of chargers.

≪ If you're not a morning person, waking up to this soothing scene could be your daybreak bliss. Grays and creams and natural surfaces mix with snowy white tulips in an earthy hand-thrown vase to ease you into the day with a whisper rather than a roar.

⅀ The faded reds in the tablecloth get called out by a pitcherful of crimson flowers to create a breakfast table eye-opener in a family-room corner. Couldn't you just see yourself snuggled in amid the cushions for a lazy Sunday morning paper-reading session?

⌃ Showing a resourcefulness typical of Manhattan apartment dwellers, a dining table gets pulled into the living room and draped in a purple burlap tablecloth for a breakfast party. A neophyte New Yorker joins the fun in her bright red highchair.

≫ A whimsical zinc rabbit adds charm to a place set for a comfy morning meal. *Furoshiki* wrapping cloths—traditional Japanese textiles used to bundle up clothes, gifts, and other goods—are double-sided, so they make exquisite napkins. A place card nestles in a miniature porcelain apple.

MORNING GLORY BRUNCH

⩔ Simple country fare matches the low-key rattan charger and white plates. A pile of peaches lets guests fill their pockets with sustenance on their way to a morning hike.

≫ Light streams in on a table set for brunch with the eye-catching color of orange parrot tulips matched by orange juice served in wine glasses. Everything needed to quickly set the table is within easy reach on the shelves to the right.

◄◄ Ceramic flowers in pots run down the center of a courtyard table. Bougainvillea petals are strewn haphazardly across the patterned tablecloth, turning the table into a symphony of pinks and greens that hits all the right chords.

⌄ The trick to making a centerpiece that's floral and gardeny, but also a little wild, is to limit your palette to three colors. Purple conveys springtime in an unexpected way, and Depression-era green glass goblets and ceramic chargers bring out the greens in the botanicals. Gold flatware adds warmth and, simply because it's not silver, brings an element of surprise.

⌃ It's hard to compete with Mother Nature, but why not give it a shot and go for all-out color? The lively floral napkins inspired this table's brave palette and keep all the hues pulled together to hold chromatic cacophony at bay.

≫ For an alfresco lunch, heirloom china is mixed with a mismatched collection of whimsical finds and a profusion of fresh flowers from the garden. Solid-color napkins give the polka-dot tablecloth more impact, and a pretty menu card provides the finishing touch.

GARDEN PARTY

⌄   A Jane Austen–worthy pastoral picnic takes full advantage of a beautiful summer day with rough-hewn logs from fallen trees in the roles of both table and chair backs.

»   Flowers, a tablecloth, and real flatware are such a luxury for outdoor dining that guests can't help but be impressed. Practicality does prevail, though—the plates are melamine, and the mint julep cups are unbreakable copperplate.

GARDEN PARTY

What could be more romantically Old South than lunch in the lee of a double porch beneath a hundred-year-old willow? No additional embellishment needed, except maybe a soft breeze to gently billow the crisp white tablecloth. Sheer elegance in the garden.

Gloriously weathered French bistro table and chairs, paired with their classical accompaniment of beige pea gravel, get vivid shots of color from Italian striped linen napkins. A leftover napkin even fills in ably as a tablecloth. Vintage pressed-glass side tables hold serving platters to preserve precious tabletop real estate.

≪ Why not show your local florist a snapshot of your china pattern and ask that they copy it in a flower arrangement? That's what this designer did for a ladies' lunch in this sun-filled garden. A low-key striped tablecloth lets the extravagant arrangement take the spotlight.

⌄ Breezy cotton linens freshen up stuffy traditional china, and the splash of a cobalt blue mug makes everything else pop.

≪ Crisp yellow-and-white runners extend vertically under place settings laid across from one another, and napkins are tied with blue-and-white ribbon. Jars filled with homemade jam serve as place-card holders.

⌄ Queen Anne's lace grows wild along many of America's northern roads; why not pull over and pick as much as you can and fill three gigantic metal urns for your alfresco fete? Fanciful faux butterflies wired into the arrangements appear to be fluttering happily above the table.

GARDEN PARTY

Why not serve up simplicity as companion to the enchanting views of this dusky dell? Going natural doesn't have to mean a sea of beige, blue makes a great base for layering. Naturally weathered chairs get a fun (and comfy!) lift from blue pillows. And soft prewashed cotton linens make an easygoing statement.

The tactile subtlety of these handmade plates pairs well with colorful food. For balance, flatware has a matte finish to keep shiny reflections to a minimum and maintain the table's feeling of peacefulness. Rather than traditional flower centerpieces, pots of herbs are scattered about inviting guests to pluck and taste while enjoying their first course of honey-drizzled cheese.

« Go all-out tropical to create a vibrant table with just a touch of campy kitsch. Alternating warm and cool hues creates interest, and varying the place settings gives guests their own special moment.

⌄ This place setting is as tropical as a toucan, right down to the serving of papaya alongside a flamingo napkin ring. An orange runner across the middle of the table provides a solid ground to all the bursts of hot color.

AN UNAPOLOGETICALLY UNINHIBITED THEME PARTY

⩔ Purple accents at this autumnal wine-tasting dinner immediately call to mind the rich red wine to come. The color green's place on the far side of the color wheel from purple always makes that chromatic combination a good bet. Concrete garden stools almost look like wine casks.

≫ The eggplants set at every seat are a three-dimensional exclamation point. The embroidered pine branches on the linen napkins pick up the greens in the tablecloth, and a brass lobster hints at the menu.

"YOU'RE ONLY GIVEN ONE LITTLE SPARK OF MADNESS. IF YOU LOSE THAT, YOU'RE NOTHIN.'"

ROBIN WILLIAMS

Talk about a sugar rush! This four-tier centerpiece was built from stacks of Styrofoam, frosted with tinted and white fondant, and embellished with all kinds of candy. Even the plates and napkins look sweet enough to eat. »

«   Easter calls for eggs, more eggs, a profusion of pastels, and champagne at lunch! A paisley tablecloth inspired some orange accents, and a low vase allows for free-flowing conversations across the table.

⌄   Gold napkin rings pick up the color of the chargers and the gold rims of the glassware, helping to harmonize the mismatched linens.

‹‹ In this African motif, wooden tigers slink around the plates and giraffes seem to nibble at the faux flowers (using artificial flowers means not being limited to what's in season). The tablecloth embroidery evokes the thorn trees and baobabs that silhouette against the grasslands of the African savanna.

⌄ Fringed napkins have a grassy, tactile feel to them, and monogrammed dessert plates are a lovely surprise at the end of a meal. Colored glass is like silver; it adds sparkle.

"THERE ARE FEW HOURS IN LIFE MORE AGREEABLE THAN THE HOUR DEDICATED TO THE CEREMONY KNOWN AS AFTERNOON TEA."

HENRY JAMES

« Give a fancy ladies' tea party, but don't go overboard with the floral prints.
This frilly, rose-strewn runner seems less sweet surrounded by mostly plain china. Patterns are
tamed by a simple white linen napkin and a loose arrangement of roses, lilacs, and peonies.
And what's with teacups and saucers anyway? Why not serve your tea in a much friendlier and less
cumbersome mug? For that matter, why not go ahead and break out the white wine?

AN UNAPOLOGETICALLY UNINHIBITED THEME PARTY

Thinking about hosting a boho-chic fiesta? Textiles collected in Mexico (or online) make great table runners, and any leftovers can serve as throws on the backs of chairs. Cacti centerpieces in colorful pots and an antique terra-cotta urn complete the south-of-the-border look.

If you mix hues seen infrequently in each other's company, such as peach tassels alongside purple napkins, your table will always feel relaxed—just right for that pitcher of margaritas with your best amigos. Tassels topping every plate provide texture and double as party favors!

CHAPTER THREE

THE ABBONDANZA BUFFET

LAY IT ALL OUT LIKE YOUR HOME IS THE KING'S BANQUETING HALL,
AND LET THEM PILE THEIR PLATES HIGH AND FILL THEIR GLASSES FULL
WHILE YOU JUST SIT BACK AND ACCEPT THE KUDOS. SERVING A BUFFET
MEANS NEVER HAVING TO SAY, "IT'S COMING!"

≪ Flowers and table linens call out the peachy hues in the antique rug, while the arrangements of small vases on the mantel feel fresh and unfussy.

(Previous Spread) Good wine, fresh produce, the scent of lavender, the pop of geraniums, a hilly vineyard view: Heaven.

⌃ Forks served up in mint julep cups mix with classic monogrammed napkins to highlight the party's beguiling mix of the casual and genteel.

≪ As summer approaches, these homeowners place pots filled with succulents and tropical plants on an eight-foot antique stone table so they're ready for spontaneous cocktail parties all season long—just add a loaf of bread, jug of wine, and your favorite group of friends.

⌃ A cocktail party in a walled patio goes fairy-tale castle with lots and lots (and lots) of candles flickering on chunky wooden candlesticks. A paisley tablecloth draped on a casual diagonal across a wood refectory table adds to the setting's baronial attitude.

>> With a view like this, who wants to go inside for a refill? At a buffet laden with good things to eat and drink, the hosts can settle in alongside their guests and watch for Sagittarius to materialize above the pergola overhead.

"DON'T BE AFRAID TO USE YOUR FINEST CHINA, SILVERWARE, AND CRYSTAL OUTDOORS. IT CAN MAKE A CASUAL EVENT A BIT MORE SPECIAL."

TY BURKS

Here's to good conversation and putting your feet up at an outdoor fireplace. Add olives, cheese, and a glass of champagne raised to friendship, and you've pretty much defined paradise. **»**

⌄ For a transporting effect, take a luscious floral tablecloth intended for indoor dining and bring it outside for some fresh air. Crisp hemstitched napkins, candlelight, and jasmine in a nineteenth-century bowl are simple, refined luxuries that your most discerning guests won't fail to appreciate.

≫ Red wine, pizza, focaccia, and pears sit in the shade of a massive camphor tree. Drape a big linen cloth over a stone table, and you've got everything you need for an idyllic Tuscan-style cocktail party.

« Mille Fleur bantam chickens scratch about the pea-gravel terrace, where an iron candelabra with black candles lends a shot of gothic romance to a cocktail party's fairy-tale pastoral setting.

⌄ Your party can effortlessly transition from brunch to dinner when magical strings of lights twinkle above your table, anticipating the night sky while the sun is up and adding a romantic glow when it goes down. The powder-blue and white palette echoes the hues of the sunroom, visible through the open French doors. The colors feel approachable; there's absolutely nothing formal or overwhelming about this setting.

DRINKS PARTY UNDER THE STARS

⌄ Why not take your predinner in plein air. If your terrace is small, just do a small bar. Simple votives, a bunch of flowers, and a limited offering of champagne and wine. *C'est parfait.*

» You don't need to hire a band to give a jazzy cocktail party. But, let's face it, it doesn't hurt!

« Sometimes, just a bottle of good champagne will do. Orange tulips and votives stand out against luxuriant black-and-white curtains and draw the eye to the serve-yourself ice bucket.

⌃ Grab a glass of champagne at the bar on the right and enjoy an old-style New Orleans jazz band.

‹‹ A brass étagère is a Billy Baldwin–style touch of class that works in every conceivable decorating scheme. Employed as a home bar and organized with reflective white lacquer trays, it has an irresistibly youthful appeal.

⌄ An 1860s refectory table features a thirty-inch-long rustic antique basket that holds "all the makings" in this convivial living room. A root mirror hints playfully at the oversized mirrors behind the shelves of potables in neighborhood taverns.

« While the facade of this custom-made bar is painted streamlined white, its interior is packed with style: high gloss aqua upper shelves set off by an ocher-and-blue paper with the warm look of cracked peanut brittle. No guest walks into a party here and has to ask where the bar is!

❯❯ A collection of colored wine and water glasses look jewel-like inside this drinks cabinet's scarlet interior. For parties the cabinet is flung wide open, with a serving table pulled alongside so guests can easily mix their own.

《 Illumination emanating from the floor and the wood shelves of this bar draws out the varied textures of terra-cotta walls and vaulted ceiling, creating an irresistible speakeasy-style hangout.

˅ A screen placed strategically behind an antique living-room console defines the designated bar area. Highball ingredients stand at the ready, practically begging guests to come help themselves.

« Two bars, no waiting! One bar holds the liquor, the other the mixers for an efficient take on self-help hospitality. A pitcher of water on the bar is always a good idea. Affordable monogrammed plastic "go" cups mix easily with fancier barware.

⌃ A deep windowsill makes a charming setting for a bar reminiscent of *A Room with a View*. Even if it's not Florence outside, a view this interesting needs no embellishment other than a pretty tray (don't forget the lemons!), some pistachios, and a selection of cut-glass barware.

"I DON'T KNOW WHY PEOPLE INSIST ON MIXING DRINKS IN THE KITCHEN. NOTHING SHOUTS 'WELCOME' LIKE A DRINKS TABLE RIGHT OUT IN THE OPEN."

JEFFREY BILHUBER

A nice way to delineate a bar is to use a tray—and why not a royally purple one at that?
Plus, trays have the additional merit of portability. Linen napkins offer an elegant alternative to paper,
and a prechilled bottle of open champagne is so enticing that even the young woman in
the artwork seems to be reaching for it. »

« Offer hospitality, not just a drink. A well-appointed bar set with attractive glassware (group colors together) is a people magnet—guests feel more at home when they can help themselves to a beverage.

⌃ A family heirloom becomes a bar cart in this dining room, where the artwork helps keep an eye on the shenanigans.

≪ You'll always be ready to get creative when you stock your bar cart with small-batch flavored syrups in addition to top-shelf liquors and mixers. A lower shelf for an ice bucket and glasses leaves room on top for garnishes like pineapples and herbs. It's niceties like these that make guests feel special!

⋎ A well-stocked midcentury bar cart follows guests from dining room to living room—wherever the party winds up.

« Lemons and limes aren't the only produce you need on your summertime bar! Try pretty pots of herbs like mint or rosemary that guests can clip and stir into their bourbon and gin. Just because something is beautiful doesn't mean it can't be useful!

⌄ When an artist works some faux-bois (literally "fake wood") magic on a bar, a closet-like space is transformed into a vivid focal point. If you don't mind a little visual deceit, it's a no brainer.

Sweetness and light prevail at a dessert party, where the square lines of a white pedestal serving platter juxtapose with a host of curvy confections. The pralines look luscious next to the pink wine glasses, and turquoise plates provide a refreshing splash of contrast.

Old-fashioned butterflies and flowers flit across plates and teacups (sometimes grandmother's china is just the thing) and a scattering of rose petals. Victoria and Albert would feel right at home with this ornate antique tray and elaborate silver forks.

"SEIZE THE MOMENT. REMEMBER ALL THOSE WOMEN ON THE *TITANIC* WHO WAVED OFF THE DESSERT CART."

ERMA BOMBECK

The after-party can look as posh as a black-tie dinner dance when the table is set with glittering plates, sterling silver, and pink and red carnations all crowded together into delightful mini bouquets. »

≪ Cupcakes are the very best kind of centerpiece—colorful, approachable, *and* edible! Pair sweet things with a teapot, a coffee carafe, and some cups like these—in such a luscious shade of brown, they could be made of chocolate themselves.

⌄ A cake stand with matching dessert plates is a bit of throwback luxury you don't see much anymore, which is precisely why it looks so chic.

DESIGNER CREDITS

PHOTOGRAPHY CREDITS

© William Abranowicz: 79

© Melanie Acevedo: 192

© Lucas Allen: 108

© Jessica Antola: 8

© Quentin Bacon: 32

© James Baigrie: 27, 50, 195

© Christopher Baker: 114, 115, 187

© Edmund Barr: 94

© Alberto Bartolomei: 150-151, 191

© Abigail Bobo: 140, 141

© James Carriere: 44-45, 138

© Paul Costello: 116-117, 166-167, 178- 181

© Beatriz da Costa: 18, 127, 193, 201

© Stephen Danelian: 152-153

© Reed Davis: 95, 173, 183

© Michael Devine: 146-147

© Trevor Dixon: 10-11

© Miki Duisterhof: 126

© Philip Ficks: back cover, 158-159

© Don Freeman: 78, 91

© Dana Gallagher: 76

Alison Gootee/Studio D: 4, 13, 25

© Gridley & Graves: 20- 21

© Alanna Hale: 107

© Nelson Hancock: 54

© Jeremy Harwell: 7

© Alec Hemer: 197

© Amy Herring: 66, 81, 133

© Bob Hiemstra: 49, 155

© Ingalls Photography: 148-149, 156-157

© Stephen Karlisch: 22-23

© Thomas Kuoh: 139

© Francesco Lagnese: 15, 35, 55, 60-61, 73, 103, 120-121, 135

© Frederic LaGrange: 189

© Nicole Lamotte: cover, 144-145

© David A. Land: 42

© Ryan Liebe: 162-163

© Pernille Loof: 105, 203

© Thomas Loof: 46, 93, 99

© Kerri McCaffety: 128, 188

© James Merrell: 131, 170

© Elie Miller: 111

© Johnny Miller: 194

© Karen R. Millet: 89

© Robert Millman: 104

© Amy Neunsinger: 53, 100-101, 174

© Ngoc Minh Ngo: 59, 64-65, 74, 84, 98, 132

© Kana Okada: 16-17, 40, 56-57, 82

© Victoria Pearson: 143, 168-169, 175, 176, 199, 202

© Tec Petaja: 177, 196

© Eric Piasecki: 70, 71, 77, 136, 184

© Eric Piasecki/OTTO: 134

© Jose Picayo: 164

© Manuel Rodriguez: 2

© Alexandra Rowley: 37, 83

© Lucy Schaeffer: 38, 43, 86-87

© Annie Schlecter: 198

© Joe Schmelzer: 68-69, 92, 119, 137, 142, 160, 185

© Tara Striano: 48, 63

© Eric Striffler: 106, 113

© Christopher Sturman: 39

© Trevor Tondro: 26, 58, 124, 125, 186

© Julie Toy: 30-31

© Luca Trovato: 34

© David Tsay: 90, 112

© Jonny Valiant: 28-29, 41, 130

© Mikkel Vang: 96

© Bjorn Wallander: 110, 122-123, 182

© Julian Wass: 109

© Simon Watson: 12

INDEX

HEARSTBOOKS

An Imprint of Sterling Publishing
1166 Avenue of the Americas
New York, NY 10036

ISBN 978-1-61837-234-5

Distributed in Canada by Sterling Publishing
c/o Canadian Manda Group, 664 Annette Street
Toronto, Ontario, M6S 2C8, Canada
Distributed in the United Kingdom by GMC Distribution Services
Castle Place, 166 High Street, Lewes, East Sussex, BN7 1XU, England
Distributed in Australia by NewSouth Books
45 Beach Street, Coogee, NSW 2034, Australia

For information about custom editions, special sales, and premium and corporate purchases,
please contact Sterling Special Sales at 800-805-5489 or specialsales@sterlingpublishing.com.

Manufactured in China

2 4 6 8 10 9 7 5 3 1

sterlingpublishing.com
housebeautiful.com

Interior design by Chris Thompson
Photography credits on page 205